SUMMER WRITING WORKBOOK

35 Summer Writing Activities for 3rd, 4th, 5th & 6th Grade

Day 7: Restaurant Review

Review a restaurant you visited recently. Fill in the blanks below.

Restaurant: _____
Location: _____
Type of food: _____
Date and time of visit: _____

Rate the following statements on a scale of **ONE to TEN**.
A rating of **one** indicates that it couldn't be worse. It's *TERRIBLE*!
A rating of **ten** indicates that it is fantastic! It couldn't be better!
Mark an "X" on each row to indicate your rating for each statement.

STATEMENT	1	2	3	4	5	6	7	8	9	10
Ease of parking										
Restaurant appearance										
First impression of the staff										
Comfort of the seating										
Cleanliness of the restaurant										
Ambiance (music, lighting, etc.)										
Friendliness of waitstaff										
Attentiveness of waitstaff										
Waitstaff's menu knowledge										
Wait time for food										
Food temperature										
Overall taste										
Overall value										
YOUR OVERALL EXPERIENCE										

Day 8: Journal Entry

Respond to the following journal prompt.

You're on a cruise during summer vacation. You wake up in the middle of the night as the ship rocks violently back and forth. Despite your growing fear, you choose to stay in bed and ride out the storm. Hours pass. Your stomach churns, and you wait.

There is an announcement from the captain.

"Due to the violent storm, we've lost communication with the rest of the world, and our navigation devices are no longer working. Prepare yourselves for an extended stay," he announces. "I pass along my deepest apologies for this unexpected turn of events," he continues. "Let's make this an adventure you'll never forget!" he says excitedly.

Who would you choose to be with if you knew you'd have an extended stay on a cruise ship? Why? What are some things you would take with you to enjoy your time? Why? How would you spend your time on the ship? Why?

©Kirsten Tulsian

© Kirsten Tulsian. All Rights Reserved.

Images and cover art created by Sarah Pecorino Illustration. All rights reserved. No part of this publication may be reproduced, distributed, or transmitted in any form or by any means. This includes photocopying, recording, or other electronic or mechanical methods without prior permission of the publisher, except in the case of brief quotations embodied in critical reviews and other noncommercial uses permitted by copyright law.

No part of this product may be used or reproduced for commercial use.

Contact the author:
Kirsten's Kaboodle
kirsten@kirstenskaboodle.com
PO Box 91193
Salt Lake City, UT 84109

TABLE OF CONTENTS:

Tips for Use	Page 5
This Book Belongs To	Page 7
Day 1: Journal Entry	Pages 9-10
Day 2: Story Starter	Pages 11-12
Day 3: Biography	Pages 13-14
Day 4: Autobiography	Pages 15-18
Day 5: Newspaper Article	Pages 19-20
Day 6: Descriptive Writing	Pages 21-22
Day 7: Restaurant Review	Pages 23-24
Day 8: Journal Entry	Pages 25-26
Day 9: Story Starter	Pages 27-28
Day 10: Opinion Writing	Pages 29-30
Day 11: Book Report	Pages 31-32
Day 12: Main Dish Recipe	Pages 33-34
Day 13: Persuasive Essay	Pages 35-36
Day 14: Narrative Writing	Pages 37-40
Day 15: Newspaper Article	Pages 41-42
Day 16: Journal Entry	Pages 43-44
Day 17: Story Starter	Pages 45-46

©Kirsten Tulsian

TABLE OF CONTENTS:

Day 18: Persuasive Essay	Pages 47-48
Day 19: Packing Lists	Pages 49-50
Day 20: How-to Essay	Pages 51-52
Day 21: Descriptive Essay	Pages 53-54
Day 22: Newspaper Article	Pages 55-56
Day 23: Opinion Writing	Pages 57-58
Day 24: Journal Entry	Pages 59-60
Day 25: Story Starter	Pages 61-62
Day 26: Book Report	Pages 63-64
Day 27: Narrative Writing	Pages 65-68
Day 28: Dessert Recipe	Pages 69-70
Day 29: Story Starter	Pages 71-72
Day 30: Journal Entry	Pages 73-74
Day 31: Restaurant Review	Pages 75-76
Day 32: Newspaper Article	Pages 77-78
Day 33: Opinion Writing	Pages 79-80
Day 34: Biography	Pages 81-82
Day 35: Journal Entry	Pages 83-84
About the Author	Page 85

TIPS FOR USE:

There may be instances when it's appropriate for children to share their responses with classmates, teachers, or caregivers. However, for children to get the most out of this workbook, I encourage you to offer an option to share or keep their responses private.

Generally, summer breaks range from 8-12 weeks. With 35 writing activities, it's best to plan for one activity every two days (3-4 activities per week). Presenting this workbook as a "summer writing challenge" is also a fun way to motivate children to complete the responses. Providing an incentive for completion is ALWAYS an encouraging bonus!

The following pages contain 35 writing activities. These include journal entries, story starters, persuasive essays, descriptive writing, restaurant reviews, narrative writing, and more!

Some activities include guidelines. Aside from those guidelines, it's best to allow children to be creative and use their imaginations. These are not intended to be evaluative writing activities (use this like a journal for writing practice instead of graded work). Children get plenty of written feedback, corrections, and critiques on writing assignments during the school year. It's summer… allow them to have fun with this!

If you have any questions, please don't hesitate to contact me at kirsten@kirstenskaboodle.com. You can also find related PDF resources at kirstenskaboodle.com.

Thank you for providing the children in your life with valuable writing opportunities and resources!

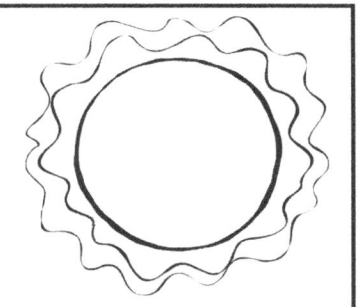

THIS BOOK BELONGS TO:

Day 1: Journal Entry

Respond to the following journal prompt.

Reflect on the school year that just ended. What was the most unexpected thing that happened? What was your involvement in this unexpected event? How did you feel about it? How did your teacher, family, friends, or community members feel about it? Is there anything related to this incident or situation that you wish you could change? If so, what? Would you consider this unexpected experience a positive one or a negative one? Why?

Day 1: Journal Entry

Day 2: Story Starter

Read the following story starter. Complete the story using the first-person point of view (pronouns: **I, me, my,** etc.).

> I couldn't rest comfortably. Was I dreaming? Could UFOs be real? I *suppose* creatures could live on other planets.
>
> With one blink, the most intense light I'd ever seen broke through the perimeter of my closed door. Blinding light.
>
> SQUEEEEEEAK! My eyeballs zeroed in on the doorknob. With a turn of the knob, and a gasp, the door swung open! There it was, glowing like the sun's light, staring straight into my eyes.

Day 2: Story Starter

Day 3: Biography

Got a favorite SUMMER GAMES ATHLETE? If not, choose a Summer Games sport. Do you enjoy basketball, hockey, rugby, cycling, golf, swimming, diving, or tennis?

Choose an athlete who's competed in that sport in the Summer Games. Use reputable sources (online encyclopedia or printed nonfiction material) to locate information about this person. Take notes on the table below. Finally, write a brief three-paragraph biography about the athlete you chose.

- **First paragraph**: Include information about the beginning of this person's life (birthplace, birthdate, the early years, etc.).
- **Second paragraph**: Include information about this person's middle years.
- **Third paragraph**: Include information about the last part of this person's life (or present day, if this person is still living).

Athlete: _____ **Sport:** _____

Birthdate: _____	Early Years: _____
Place of Birth: _____	_____
Date of Death: _____	_____
Interesting Facts: _____	_____
_____	_____
_____	_____
_____	_____
Middle Years: _____	Current or Later Years: _____
_____	_____
_____	_____
_____	_____
_____	_____
_____	_____

©Kirsten Tulsian

Day 3: Biography

Day 4: Autobiography

NOTE: USE PAGES 15-18 FOR THIS WRITING ACTIVITY!

An autobiography is a story about your own life (written by you). If you get stuck, use these questions to help you complete it. It's best if events are sequential (start from the beginning of your life and describe events as they happened up to the present day).

- Date and place of your birth (city, state, and country)
- Names of parents and siblings (as well as ages of siblings)
- Where you grew up
- Pets (types of pets and their names)
- Significant memories or events
- Funny stories
- Places you've visited
- Things you've learned
- Information about your friends
- Scary moments
- Accomplishments
- Family memories
- Your favorite food, color, game, TV show, movie, activity, sport, or toy growing up
- Your hopes, dreams, and fears for the future

_____

_____

_____

_____

_____

_____

_____

Day 4: Autobiography

Day 4: Autobiography

Day 4: Autobiography

Write a newspaper article about a significant event happening during summer vacation. Include details (Who? What? When? Where? Why? How?).

Day 5

Summer Shenanigans

TOP STORY!

Date:

Title:

Written By: _____

Caption:

Day 5

Title:

Caption:

Caption:

Day 6: Descriptive Writing

TOPIC: Describe your favorite place in the world.

Fill in the table below. Then write a descriptive essay. Remember to include a variety of adjectives to create a vivid picture in the reader's mind. Use figurative language, such as similes, metaphors, onomatopoeia, and personification.

I smell…	I hear…
I feel…	I see…

Other descriptive words or phrases:

©Kirsten Tulsian

Day 6: Descriptive Writing

Day 7: Restaurant Review

Review a restaurant you visited recently. Fill in the blanks below.

Restaurant: _____

Location: _____

Type of food: _____

Date and time of visit: _____

Rate the following statements on a scale of **ONE to TEN**.

A rating of **one** indicates that it couldn't be worse. It's *TERRIBLE*!

A rating of **ten** indicates that it is fantastic! It couldn't be better!

Mark an "X" on each row to indicate your rating for each statement.

STATEMENT	1	2	3	4	5	6	7	8	9	10
Ease of parking										
Restaurant appearance										
First impression of the staff										
Comfort of the seating										
Cleanliness of the restaurant										
Ambiance (music, lighting, etc.)										
Friendliness of waitstaff										
Attentiveness of waitstaff										
Waitstaff's menu knowledge										
Wait time for food										
Food temperature										
Overall taste										
Overall value										
YOUR OVERALL EXPERIENCE										

©Kirsten Tulsian

Day 7: Restaurant Review

Write a review of your chosen restaurant.
What did you like about the restaurant? What could be improved? Do you recommend this restaurant to others? Why or why not?

Day 8: Journal Entry

Respond to the following journal prompt.

You're on a cruise during summer vacation. You wake up in the middle of the night as the ship rocks violently back and forth. Despite your growing fear, you choose to stay in bed and ride out the storm. Hours pass. Your stomach churns, and you wait.

There is an announcement from the captain.

"Due to the violent storm, we've lost communication with the rest of the world, and our navigation devices are no longer working. Prepare yourselves for an extended stay," he announces. "I pass along my deepest apologies for this unexpected turn of events," he continues. "Let's make this an adventure you'll never forget!" he says excitedly.

Who would you choose to be with if you knew you'd have an extended stay on a cruise ship? Why? What are some things you would take with you to enjoy your time? Why? How would you spend your time on the ship? Why?

Day 8: Journal Entry

Day 9: Story Starter

Read the following story starter. Complete the story using the first-person point of view (pronouns: **I, me, my,** etc.).

> Like magnets, my feet inched closer to the bathtub's drain. The pulling sensation was intense. As the tub emptied, a whirlpool formed above the drain. It pulled me closer as it gained strength. I grasped the sides of the bathtub as my body slid closer and closer to the drain. As I took a deep breath, I felt my toes slip into the drain's opening.
>
> In the blink of an eye, the bathtub was empty.
>
> As if on a waterslide, I slid through the drainpipe until it spat me out at the other end. It wasn't long before I realized I'd entered a beautiful new dimension. The first thing that caught my eye was…

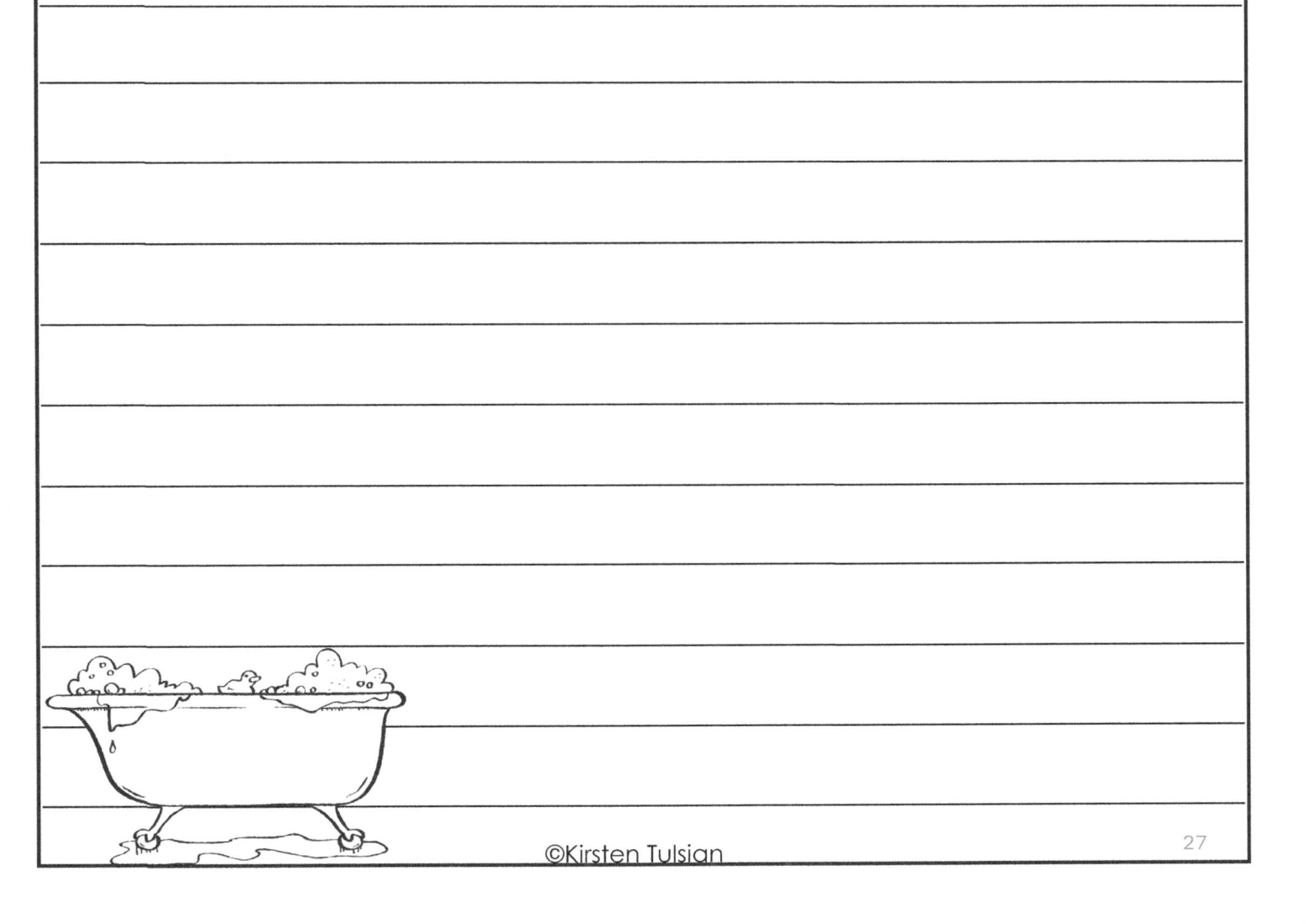

Day 9: Story Starter

Day 10: Opinion Writing

Topic Choices:
- **The best summer activity**
- **The worst summer chore**

Choose a topic from the options above. Then, fill in the graphic organizer below. Finally, write an essay explaining your opinion. Remember to begin each paragraph with a topic sentence. Follow it with supporting details and/or explanations.

- First paragraph: State your opinion. Provide support for your opinion.
- Second paragraph: Explain and support your second reason.
- Third paragraph: Explain and support your third reason.

Opinion Statement:
Reason #1:
Reason #2:
Reason #3:

©Kirsten Tulsian

Day 10: Opinion Writing

Day 11: Book Report

Choose a book you read in the last year. Fill in the graphic organizer below and use that information to write a book report. Include a summary of the book as well as your own thoughts, reactions, and feelings. Remember to begin each paragraph with a topic sentence, followed by supporting details.

Book Title:	
Author:	
Genre:	
Setting:	
Characters:	
Plot:	
Favorite Part:	

Day 11: Book Report

Day 12: Main Dish Recipe

Day 12

Choose one of your favorite summer meals. If you don't know the ingredients or cooking instructions, ask an adult to help you. You can also search for it online or in a recipe book. Use that information to help you complete this recipe writing activity. Remember that this should be a main course for breakfast, lunch, or dinner. Many times, when it's hot outside, a cold meal is best!

Name of Dish:
This recipe serves _____ people.
Preparation Time: _____ minutes
Ingredients:
Notes:

Day 12: Main Dish Recipe

Directions:

Day 13: Persuasive Essay

Do you think kids should have homework during summer vacation? Why or why not? Persuade your audience.

Position or Opinion:	**Reasons:**
I believe that...	1. 2. 3.
Evidence or Examples:	You might argue that _____, but...

Begin your persuasive essay below. Continue writing on the next page.

Day 13: Persuasive Essay

Day 14: Narrative Writing

NOTE: USE PAGES 37-40 FOR THIS WRITING ACTIVITY!

Narrative writing is a type of writing that tells a story. This type of writing includes the following elements:

- **CHARACTER(S)**- the people, animals, or creatures in the story
- **SETTING**- the location of the story
- **PLOT**- a series of events that includes a beginning, a middle, and an end
- **CONFLICT**- a struggle or challenge experienced by the main character(s)

Choose one of the following topics. Then, fill in the graphic organizer and write your narrative story.

1. Imagine you wake up one summer morning to find that you've switched places with your dog. Write a story about your adventures (don't forget to include a conflict).
2. It's a beautiful summer evening. You're staring at the moon. Suddenly, the moon begins to speak. "You have ONE wish! What will it be?" it says. You tell the moon about your wish, and much to your surprise, it immediately comes true. Write a story about what happens next (don't forget to include a conflict).

Story Title:

Characters:

Setting:

Beginning:	Conflict:
Middle:	
End:	

Day 14: Narrative Writing

Day 14: Narrative Writing

Day 14: Narrative Writing

Write a newspaper article about something that impacted your community recently. What happened? How did it impact your community? As a result of this incident, how will the future be different?

Day 15

Community Chronicle
BREAKING NEWS!

Date: _____

Title: _____

Written By: _____

Caption: _____

Day 15

Title:

Caption:

Caption:

42 ©Kirsten Tulsian

Day 16: Journal Entry

Respond to the following journal prompt.

Yahoo! You get to plan a week-long summer camp! First, choose the location of the summer camp (it can be anywhere in the world). Next, plan the daily activities for the kids in the camp as well as any field trips outside the camp area. Describe what you would do each day (beginning on Monday and ending on Friday). If there is a special reason you chose any of the activities, please explain.

Day 16: Journal Entry

Day 17: Story Starter

Read the following story starter. Complete the story using the third-person point of view (pronouns: **he, she, they,** etc.).

Julian pulled the shower curtain back to reveal the source of the splashing and squealing coming from the bathtub.

Startled, a little green creature jumped up and down under the faucet.

"AAAAAH!" Julian shrieked as he quickly threw the curtain back.

"Wait! Don't be afraid! Please! I'm just trying to get cleaned up!" squealed the high-pitched voice.

Baffled, Julian peeked around the curtain to take another look. His mouth gaped open. Where did this cute little creature come from?

"Can you help me out? I can't reach the knob for the hot water, and it's cold in here," the 6-inch creature barked.

Day 17: Story Starter

Day 18: Persuasive Essay

Do you think kids should be able to decorate the walls in their bedroom in any way they choose (including painting, drawing, etc.)? Why or why not? Persuade your audience.

Position or Opinion: I believe that…	**Reasons:** 1. 2. 3.
Evidence or Examples:	You might argue that _____, but…

Begin your persuasive essay below. Continue writing on the next page.

_____
_____
_____
_____
_____
_____

Day 18: Persuasive Essay

_____
_____
_____
_____
_____
_____
_____
_____
_____
_____
_____
_____

If I could paint or draw on my bedroom wall, it would look like this...

Day 19: Packing Lists

Packing Lists: Where are you going? How long are you staying? Think about where you might be going in the future and create a list for that adventure. Pick four destinations and make a packing list for each one. Some examples might include: a sleepover with a friend, a weekend getaway to grandma's house, a weekend trip to the beach, a camping trip, or a one-day trip to the lake.

Destination: _____

Length of Stay: _____

List of Items:

Destination: _____

Length of Stay: _____

List of Items:

Day 19: Packing Lists

Destination: _____

Length of Stay: _____

List of Items:

Destination: _____

Length of Stay: _____

List of Items:

Day 20: How-To Essay

My Favorite Summer Game or Sport: How to PLAY!

Choose your favorite summer game or sport (soccer, volleyball, basketball, cornhole, croquet, tennis, baseball, lacrosse, etc.). Fill in the table below and write a how-to essay on the lines. Remember to use transition words such as first, next, then, during, last, and finally. Make sure to add the game rules to your essay.

NOTE: Pretend you're teaching someone who has never seen or heard about this game or sport. Be as specific as possible in your explanation.

Summer Game or Sport:

Equipment:

Object of the game/sport:

Rules:

Day 20: How-To Essay

Day 21: Descriptive Essay

TOPIC CHOICES:
- **Describe a summer thunderstorm.**
- **Describe a sunset walk on the beach.**

Fill in the table below. Then write a descriptive essay. Remember to include a variety of adjectives to create a picture in the reader's mind. Use figurative language, such as similes, metaphors, onomatopoeia, and personification.

I smell…	I hear…
I feel…	I see…

Other descriptive words or phrases:

_____
_____
_____
_____
_____
_____
_____
_____

Day 21: Descriptive Essay

You just broke a Guinness World Record! What did you do?
NOTE: Use your own name. Write this article in the third-person point of view (pronouns include **he, she, him, her**, etc.).

Day 22

World Record Round-Up
HEAR YE! HEAR YE!
Date:

Title:

Written By: _____

Caption:

Day 22

Title:

Caption:

Caption:

56 ©Kirsten Tulsian

Day 23: Opinion Writing

Topic Choices:
- **The best sport to play in the summer**
- **The best season (summer, fall, winter, or spring)**

Choose a topic from the options above. Then, fill in the graphic organizer below. Finally, write an essay explaining your opinion. Remember to begin each paragraph with a topic sentence. Follow it with supporting details and/or explanations.

- First paragraph: State your opinion. Provide support for your opinion.
- Second paragraph: Explain and support your second reason.
- Third paragraph: Explain and support your third reason.

Opinion Statement:
Reason #1:
Reason #2:
Reason #3:

Day 23: Opinion Writing

Day 24: Journal Entry

Respond to the following journal prompt.

Summer is a perfect time to reflect on the things you are grateful for. Create a list of 25 things that bring you joy and happiness. They can be simple things like markers and paper, or more elaborate things like freedom, the love and support from your family or your education. Try to include simple pleasures that people take for granted.

"Gratitude turns what we have into enough."
-Melody Beattie

Day 24: Journal Entry

It is not happy people who are thankful. It is thankful people who are happy.

Day 25: Story Starter

Read the following story starter. Complete the story using the first-person point of view (pronouns: **I, me, my,** etc.).

Last week, my life turned upside down. Actually, ahem, let me clarify. It didn't turn upside down; it stayed upright, but let's say my perspective changed. You see, I woke up last Friday, and I was 23½ feet tall. Yes, you read that right. If I stacked my old 4½ foot self end-to-end more than FIVE times, I would be my new height. Folded in half at my waist, I woke up on my bedroom floor with every limb rammed into the walls and furniture. *That* is when the shenanigans began.

©Kirsten Tulsian

Day 25: Story Starter

Day 26: Book Report

Choose a book you read in the last year. Fill in the graphic organizer below and use that information to write a book report. Include a summary of the book as well as your own thoughts, reactions, and feelings. Remember to begin each paragraph with a topic sentence, followed by supporting details.

Book Title:
Author:
Genre:
Setting:
Characters:
Plot:
Favorite Part:

_____
_____
_____
_____
_____

Day 26: Book Report

Day 27: Narrative Writing

NOTE: USE PAGES 65-68 FOR THIS WRITING ACTIVITY!

Narrative writing is a type of writing that tells a story. This type of writing includes the following elements:

- **CHARACTER(S)**- the people, animals, or creatures in the story
- **SETTING**- the location of the story
- **PLOT**- a series of events that includes a beginning, a middle, and an end
- **CONFLICT**- a struggle or challenge experienced by the main character(s)

Choose one of the following topics. Then, fill in the graphic organizer and write your narrative story.

1. Imagine getting a letter in the mail announcing your BIG WIN! You get to choose any superpower in the world and use it to make the world a better place. Write a story about your new superpower and all the ways you can improve the lives of others.
2. You find a coin on the ground while walking to school. The second you slide it into your pocket, strange things begin to happen. Write a story about what happens to you. How does this magic coin change your life?

Story Title:

Characters:

Setting:

Beginning:	Conflict:
Middle:	
End:	

Day 27: Narrative Writing

Day 27: Narrative Writing

Day 27: Narrative Writing

Day 28: Dessert Recipe

Choose one of your favorite SUMMER desserts. If you don't know the ingredients or the baking instructions, ask an adult to help you. You can also search online or in a recipe book. Use that information to help you complete this writing activity. Remember, this should be a dessert, such as pie, cake, or cobbler. Many summer favorites don't even need to be baked and are best served cold!

Name of dessert:
This recipe serves _____ people.
Preparation Time: _____ minutes
Ingredients:
Notes:

Day 28: Dessert Recipe

Directions:

Day 29: Story Starter

Read the following story starter. Complete the story using the first-person point of view (pronouns: **I, me, my,** etc.).

As soon as I opened my book, a cold gust of air enveloped my face. Despite my greatest efforts to keep them open, my eyes closed. Spinning, spinning, spinning… as dizzy as a towel in the spin cycle of the washing machine, I managed to crack my right eye open just a sliver.

Hot diggity dog, I was there! I was in the book! My favorite book! Hold on to your socks! This is a tale of the unbelievable adventures in my favorite story.

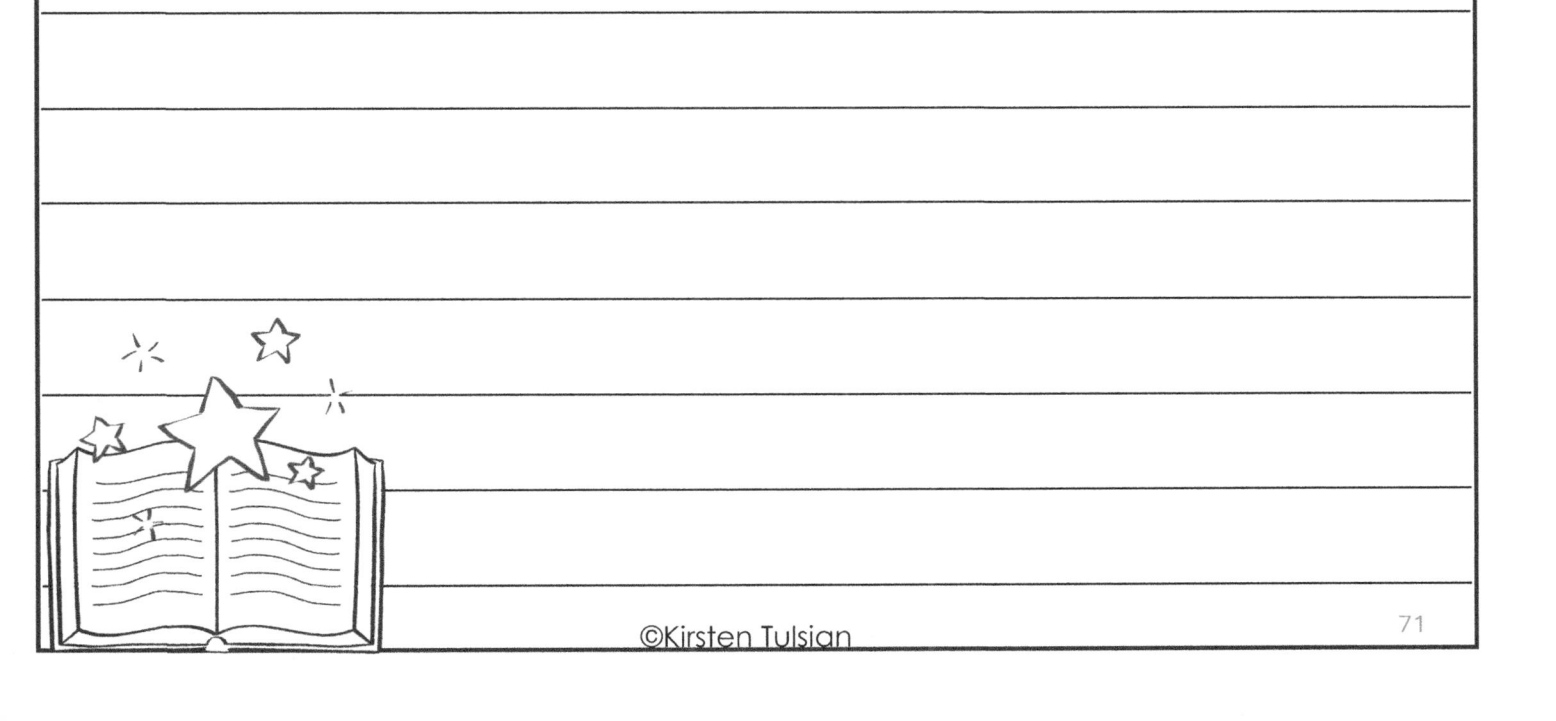

Day 29: Story Starter

Day 30: Journal Entry

Respond to the following journal prompt.

Imagine you get to inhabit the body of any animal in the wild. Which animal would you choose? Why? What would you do all day and all night long? How would you interact with your habitat and the other animals? How would you find food and water? Provide vivid details to create a picture in the mind of your readers.

Day 30: Journal Entry

Day 31: Restaurant Review

Review a restaurant you visited recently. Fill in the blanks below.

Restaurant: _____

Location: _____

Type of food: _____

Date and time of visit: _____

Rate the following statements on a scale of **ONE to TEN**.

A rating of **one** indicates that it couldn't be worse. It's *TERRIBLE*!

A rating of **ten** indicates that it is fantastic! It couldn't be better!

Mark an "X" on each row to indicate your rating for each statement.

STATEMENT	1	2	3	4	5	6	7	8	9	10
Ease of parking										
Restaurant appearance										
First impression of the staff										
Comfort of the seating										
Cleanliness of the restaurant										
Ambiance (music, lighting, etc.)										
Friendliness of waitstaff										
Attentiveness of waitstaff										
Waitstaff's menu knowledge										
Wait time for food										
Food temperature										
Overall taste										
Overall value										
YOUR OVERALL EXPERIENCE										

©Kirsten Tulsian

Day 31: Restaurant Review

Write a review of your chosen restaurant.
What did you like about the restaurant? What could be improved? Do you recommend this restaurant to others? Why or why not?

Write a newspaper article about a product you LOVE (a household, clothing, wellness, beauty, or health item). Include details. Why is it so amazing? Where do you purchase it? How has it changed your life?

Day 32

The Product Promoter

GET IT NOW!

Date:

Title:

Written By: _____

Caption:

©Kirsten Tulsian

Day 32

Title:

Caption:

Product in Use Caption:

Day 33: Opinion Writing

Topic Choices:
- **Should kids get a weekly or monthly allowance?**
- **Should recycling (paper, plastic, and/glass) be mandatory?**

Choose a topic from the options above. Then, fill in the graphic organizer below. Finally, write an essay explaining your opinion. Remember to begin each paragraph with a topic sentence. Follow it with supporting details and/or explanations.

- First paragraph: State your opinion. Provide support for your opinion.
- Second paragraph: Explain and support your second reason.
- Third paragraph: Explain and support your third reason.

Opinion Statement:
Reason #1:
Reason #2:
Reason #3:

Day 33: Opinion Writing

Day 34: Biography

Got a favorite **INVENTOR**? If not, choose an inventor who's impacted your life. How did their invention change the world?

Use reputable sources (online encyclopedia or printed nonfiction material) to locate information about this person. Take notes on the table below. Finally, write a brief three-paragraph biography about the person you chose.

- **First paragraph**: Include information about the beginning of this person's life (birthplace, birthdate, the early years, etc.).
- **Second paragraph**: Include information about this person's middle years.
- **Third paragraph**: Include information about the last part of this person's life (or present day, if this person is still living).

Inventor: _____ **Invention:** _____

Birthdate: _____

Place of Birth: _____

Date of Death: _____

Interesting Facts: _____
_____
_____
_____

Early Years: _____
_____
_____
_____
_____

Middle Years: _____
_____
_____
_____
_____

Current or Later Years: _____
_____
_____
_____
_____

Day 34: Biography

Day 35: Journal Entry

Respond to the following journal prompt.

If you could trade places with any living human in a position of power today, who would it be? Explain two reasons you chose this person. What would you do with that power? How would you want this power to impact you? Your family? The world?

Day 35: Journal Entry

About the Author:

Kirsten Tulsian is a former elementary teacher and school counselor of 18 years. She has a Bachelor's Degree in Psychology and Elementary Education from the University of Iowa and a Master's Degree in School Counseling from Sam Houston State University. As the owner of Kirsten's Kaboodle, she is passionate about nurturing kids in heart and mind. She currently resides in Salt Lake City, where she creates social-emotional learning and language arts activities and resources for parents and educators. You can find her at kirstenskaboodle.com.

Join her email list for free PDF resources, tips, updates, and important information:
kirstenskaboodle.com/subscribe

Interested in additional workbooks created by this author?

Scan the QR code below:

Made in the USA
Las Vegas, NV
27 May 2025